D1737311

ABDO
Publishing Company

Dancing

MOVE YOUR BODY

A Kid's Guide to Fitness

A Buddy Book by Sarah Tieck

Buddy BOOKS
Move Your Body

VISIT US AT
www.abdopublishing.com

Published by ABDO Publishing Company, PO Box 398166, Minneapolis, MN 55439.

Printed in the United States of America, North Mankato, Minnesota.
092012
012013

 PRINTED ON RECYCLED PAPER

Coordinating Series Editor: Rochelle Baltzer
Contributing Editors: Stephanie Hedlund, Marcia Zappa
Graphic Design: Jenny Christensen
Cover Photograph: *Shutterstock*: holbox.
Interior Photographs/Illustrations: *AP Photo*: ABC, Adam Larkey (p. 11); *Eighth Street Studio* (p. 26); *Getty Images*: David Handley (p. 19), Ruth Jenkinson (p. 23), Mike Lawrie (p. 5); *Glow Images*: Superstock (p. 13), Jochen Tack/ImageCroker (p. 30); *iStockphoto*: ©iStockphoto.com/bowdenimages (p. 27), ©iStockphoto.com/CEFutcher (p. 9), ©iStockphoto.com/craftvision (p. 25), ©iStockphoto.com/jeancliclac (p. 7), ©iStockphoto.com/omgimages (p. 29), ©iStockphoto.com/vgajic (p. 23); *Shutterstock*: Ariwasabi (p. 19), Ayakovlev (p. 15), caimacanul (p. 26), CHRISTIAN DE ARAUJO (p. 19), DM7 (p. 15), Inga Ivanova (p. 7), Serhiy Kyrychenko (p. 30), Lorraine Swanson (p. 17); *Thinkstock*: Goodshoot RF (p. 25), Purestock (p. 21).

Library of Congress Cataloging-in-Publication Data

Tieck, Sarah, 1976-
  Dancing / Sarah Tieck.
     p. cm. -- (Move your body: a kid's guide to fitness)
  ISBN 978-1-61783-561-2
1. Dance--Juvenile literature. I. Title.
  GV1596.5.T6 2013
  793.3--dc23
                          2012025989

Table of Contents

Healthy Living

Your body is amazing! A healthy body helps you feel good and live well. In order to be healthy, you must take care of yourself. One way to do this is to move your body.

Regular movement gives you **energy** and makes you stronger. Many kinds of exercise can help you do this. One fun type of exercise is dancing! Let's learn more about dancing.

Children should get 60 minutes of movement every day. Dancing is one way to do this.

Dancing 101

Dancers move their bodies in a **rhythmic** way. They turn and jump using their feet and legs. They shake their hips and wave their hands and arms. And, they bend and twist their waists and backs.

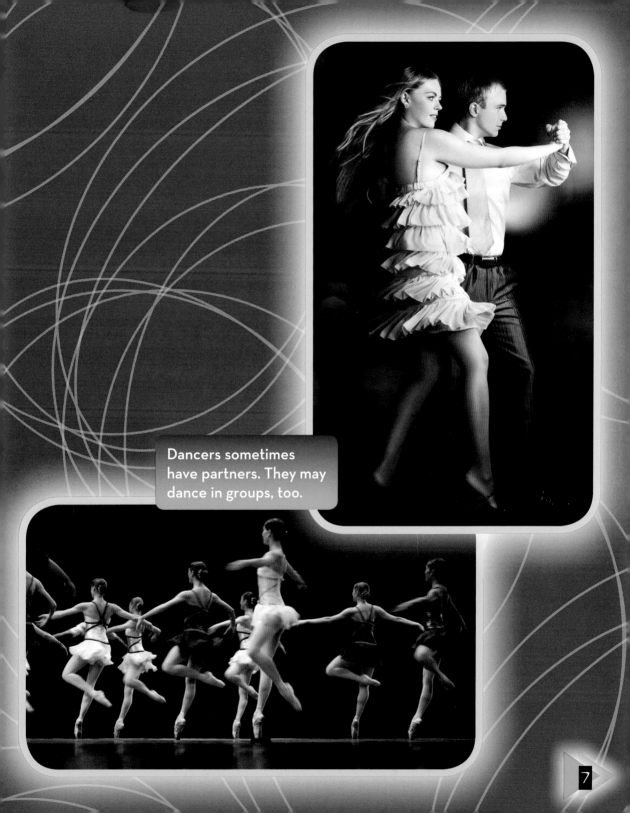

Dancers sometimes have partners. They may dance in groups, too.

Dances can be long or short. They can also be fast or slow. Dancers usually move to music. Different kinds of dancing include ballet, tap, jazz, hip-hop, folk, and ballroom. Some people do aerobic dance workouts.

Sometimes, dancers make up steps as they go. Other times, they practice many hours to learn dances. Then, they may perform on their own, with a group, or with a partner.

Zumba is a popular Latin dance workout.

Just Dance

People dance for many reasons. Some do it just for fun. Others do it as a workout. People dance as a form of art or to express their feelings. Some do it for their job. Others dance as part of contests.

Dancing can be very meaningful. Some people dance to show their beliefs. Others do it as part of their culture, or way of life.

Dancing with the Stars is a popular dance contest show on television.

Let's Get Physical

People exercise to stay fit. Regular exercise makes it easier for you to bend and move. And, it helps you stay at a healthy body weight. It also helps prevent health problems later in life.

Dancing can be a type of aerobic exercise. Some dances make your lungs and heart work hard to get your body more oxygen. The more often you exercise, the easier it will be to breathe and move.

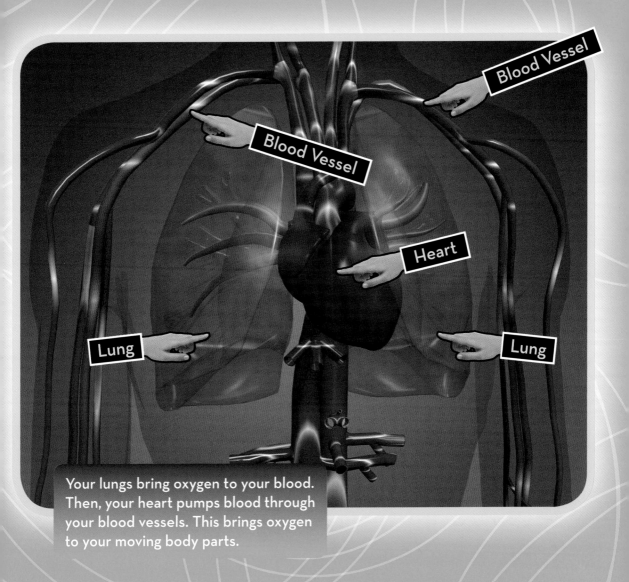

Blood Vessel

Blood Vessel

Heart

Lung

Lung

Your lungs bring oxygen to your blood. Then, your heart pumps blood through your blood vessels. This brings oxygen to your moving body parts.

Dancing also builds your **muscles**. Jumping, kicking, and turning work your leg muscles. Many movements also work your abdominal, back, and arm muscles.

Over time, your muscles will get stronger and you'll become more **flexible**. Dancers also work on balance. Some are strong and steady enough to lift others as part of a dance!

WORD OF MOUTH

Some football players do ballet! This helps them with balance and movement during games.

Abdominal Muscles

Quadriceps

Dancers need strong leg, back, and abdominal muscles.

Back Muscles

Hamstring Muscles

Calf Muscle

Gearing Up

To dance, wear comfortable clothes that you can move in easily. For most types of dancing, you'll wear special shoes on your feet. There are different outfits and shoes for different kinds of dance.

Tap shoes have metal plates on the bottom. They make sounds when you move your feet on the floor.

WORD OF MOUTH

Comfortable shoes that fit well are important for dancers. These protect the feet.

People may wear workout clothes to do **aerobic** dance. Ballet dancers often wear tights, leotards, and ballet shoes. Ballroom, theatrical, and folk dancers wear costumes to put on a show.

Aerobic Dance ➡

⬅ **Ballet**

Folk Dance ➡

Play It Safe

Dancers may get hurt. Sometimes dancing can make **muscles** sore. Dancers can have problems with their feet and legs. So, it is important to be careful when you dance.

When dancers get hurt, they need to rest so their bodies can heal.

One way to stay safe is to prepare your muscles to work hard. Before dancing, warm up by slowly moving your arms and legs. Slow movements help warm up your heart and lungs, too.

After dancing, cool down by moving slowly to help prevent sore muscles. Careful stretching is also an important part of exercise. Over time, this makes you more flexible.

Dancers often stretch after their warm up and after their workouts.

Ready? Set? Go!

Anyone can dance! All you have to do is move your body in a **rhythmic** way. Try turning on the radio and moving to the beat of the music.

If you want to learn a certain style of dancing, take a class. You'll learn more about proper form as well as safety tips.

When dancers are learning new moves, it is helpful to have a teacher watch.

Brain Food

How do you know if you are dancing hard enough to get a workout?

People who dance for their workout often measure their heart rate. This is the number of times your heart beats per minute.

A tool called a heart rate monitor measures this. You can also find it on your own. Touch the inside of your wrist. Then, count the pulses you feel in one minute.

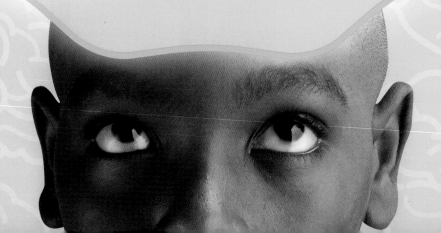

I don't know how to dance. Is there a way to learn besides taking classes?

You can learn to dance by doing moves in front of your mirror. You could also try out dances you see on television, on the Internet, or in movies. The more you practice, the better you'll become!

What is the best food to eat for dancing?

Sometimes dancers avoid food in order to stay thin. This is not a good choice. Your body needs the right amount of food from all of the food groups. So, eat plenty of fruits, vegetables, lean proteins, dairy, and whole grains.

Choose to Move

Remember that dancing makes your body stronger. Fitness is an important part of a healthy life. Dance as often as you can. Each positive choice you make will help you stay healthy.

There is no one way to dance. Dancing can be playful and fun!

STRETCH OUT

✔ Dancers may do high kicks. Stretching your leg **muscles** and joints can make these easier.

✔ Over time, bending over and touching your toes can help you move more easily.

JUST DO IT

✔ Water plays an important part in helping your body build muscle. So, be sure to drink some before, during, and after dancing.

✔ Dancers may get sweaty while working on a dance. Be sure to take a shower afterward so your body doesn't smell.

WORK IT

✔ Set a **goal** to improve your dancing. You could try learning a new move!

✔ Work out by playing a dance video game!

Important Words

aerobic (ehr-OH-bihk) relating to exercise that increases oxygen in the body and makes the heart better able to use oxygen.

energy (EH-nuhr-jee) the power or ability to do things.

flexible able to bend or move easily.

goal something that a person works to reach or complete.

lungs body parts that help the body breathe.

muscle (MUH-suhl) body tissue, or layers of cells, that helps move the body.

oxygen (AHK-sih-juhn) a colorless gas that humans and animals need to breathe.

perform to do something in front of an audience.

protein (PROH-teen) an important part of the diet of all animals.

rhythmic (RIHTH-mihk) having a strong, regular, repeated pattern of movement or sound.

Web Sites

To learn more about dancing, visit ABDO Publishing Company online. Web sites about dancing are featured on our Book Links page. These links are routinely monitored and updated to provide the most current information available.

www.abdopublishing.com

Index